Story Book

By Julie Haydon

Illustrations by Pat Reynolds and Rachel Tonkin

T0342732

Contents

Taffy Cat

Taffy Cat's favourite place to sleep was on Angela's bed. The big, soft bed was next to a window. Taffy knew just where to lie to feel the afternoon sunshine on her fur.

One day, Angela did not get out of bed. Taffy waited and waited for her breakfast, but Angela did not get up.

Angela was very ill.

The next day, Taffy watched while strangers took Angela away on a small bed with wheels.

They put Angela in a big, white van.

Another stranger tried to take Taffy away, but Taffy was too quick for him. She ran quickly outside and onto the street.

Taffy became very thin and hungry while she waited for Angela to come back. Angela did not return to her house, so Taffy looked for a new home.

Taffy visited lots of houses.

Sometimes people gave Taffy some scraps to eat, but nobody wanted her to live in their house.

One day, Taffy saw a woman outside a small house.

Taffy weaved in and out of the woman's legs.

The woman stroked Taffy gently and let Taffy come inside. She gave Taffy some fresh fish to eat.

Soon, Taffy's favourite place to sleep was on Melissa's sofa. The big, soft sofa was under a window. Taffy knew just where to lie to feel the afternoon sunshine on her fur.

Make a Story Book

Goal

To make your own story book.

Materials

You will need:

- sheets of paper

- pencils

- an eraser

- a stapler.

Steps

1. Decide what you want to write about.

2. Plan your story by writing a few words to describe:
   - the introduction to your story
   - the problem the main character faces in your story
   - how the problem is solved.

Story idea:
A cat that needs a new home.

The introduction:
A cat is living happily with an elderly woman.

The problem:
The elderly woman gets sick and is taken to hospital.
The cat can't stay in the house.

The solution:
The cat finds a new home.

3. Start writing your story.

4. Check your story has an introduction, a problem and a solution.

One day, Taffy saw a woman outside
a small house.
Taffy weaved in and out of the woman's legs.
The woman stroked Taffy gently and let
Taffy come inside.
She gave Taffy some fresh fish to eat.

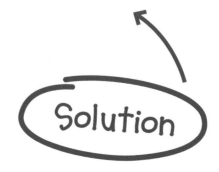

Solution

5. Read your story and correct any mistakes.
6. Use a dictionary to check the spelling of difficult words.
7. Check each sentence begins with a capital letter.
8. Check each sentence ends with a full stop.
9. Take out any words that you do not need.

Taffy Cat

One day, Angela did ~~not~~ not get out of bed. T
~~t~~affy waited and waited ~~four~~ for her breakfast, but Angela did not get up.

10. Think about the pictures you want in your story book.

11. Draw your pictures.

One day, Angela did not get out of bed. Taffy waited and waited for her breakfast, but Angela did not get up.

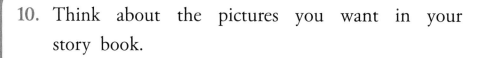

12. Draw a picture for the front cover of your story book.

13. Give your story book a title.

14. Write the title and your name on the front cover.

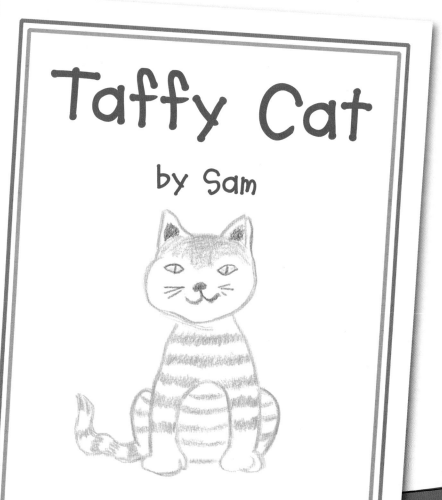

15. Staple the pages of your story book together.

16. Give your story book to your teacher, parents and friends to read.